Jon Scieszka's Trucktown

Oh No!

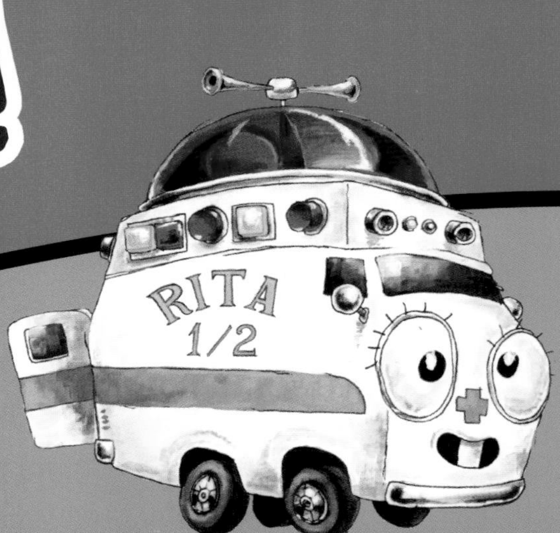

Rita

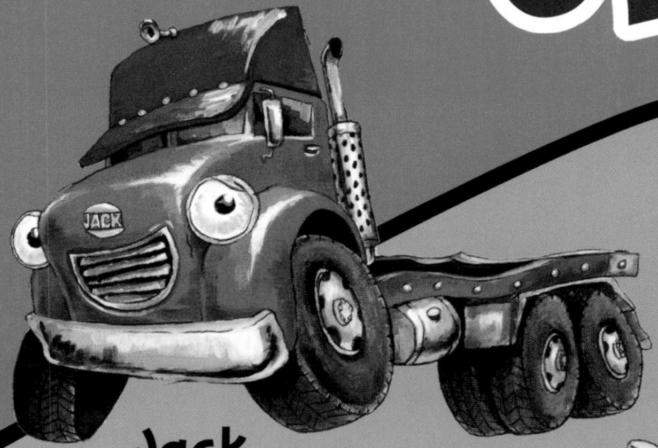

Jack

Ted

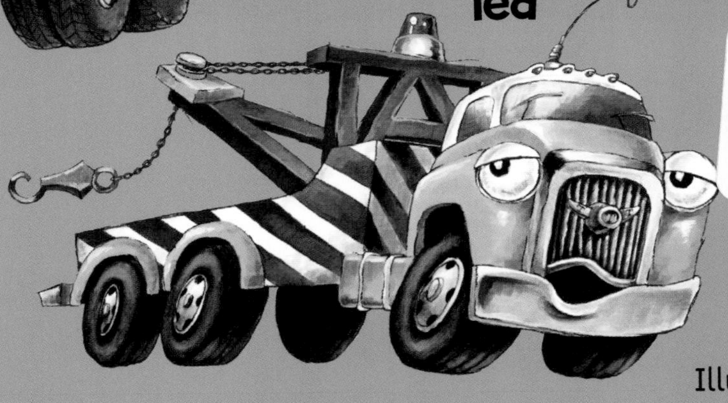

T0386053

Adapted by Alison Hawes

Illustrated by Design Garage

Snow

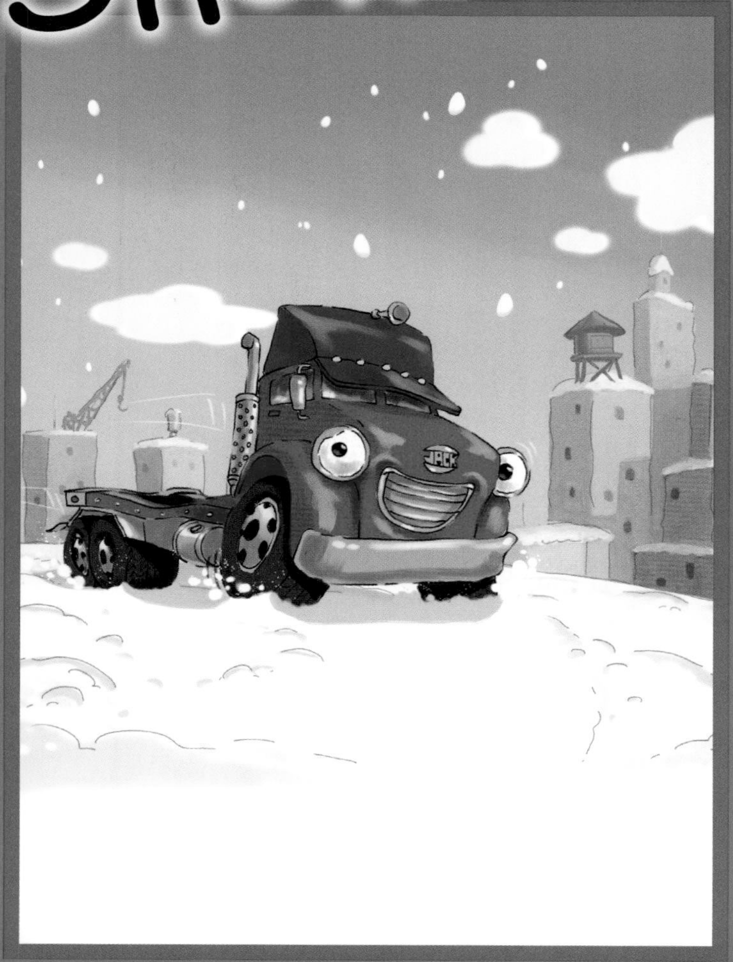

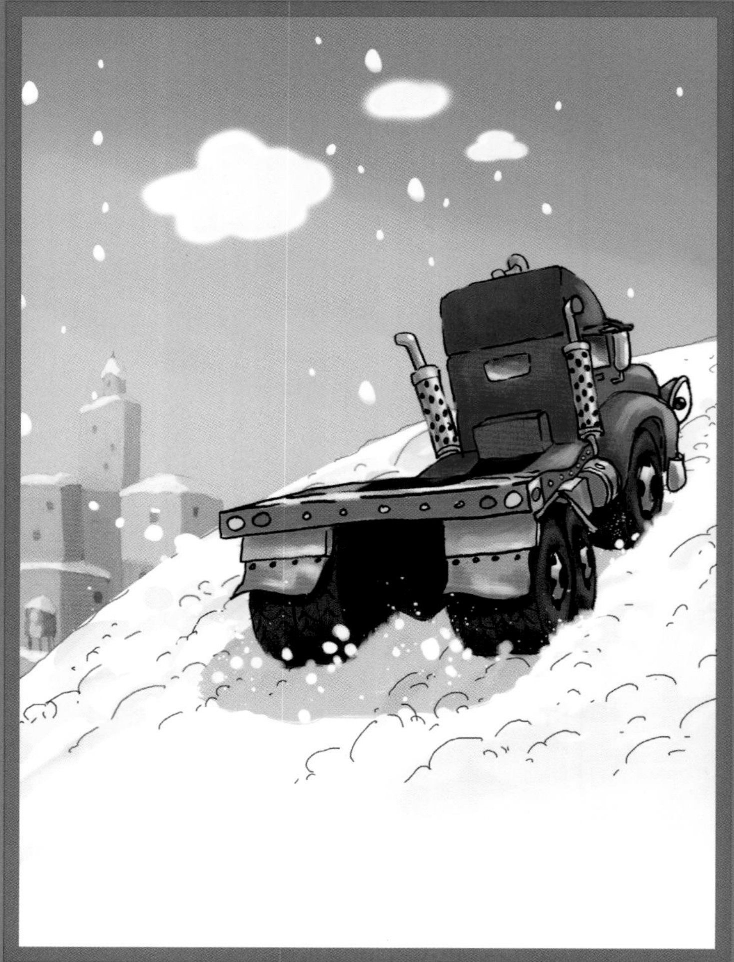

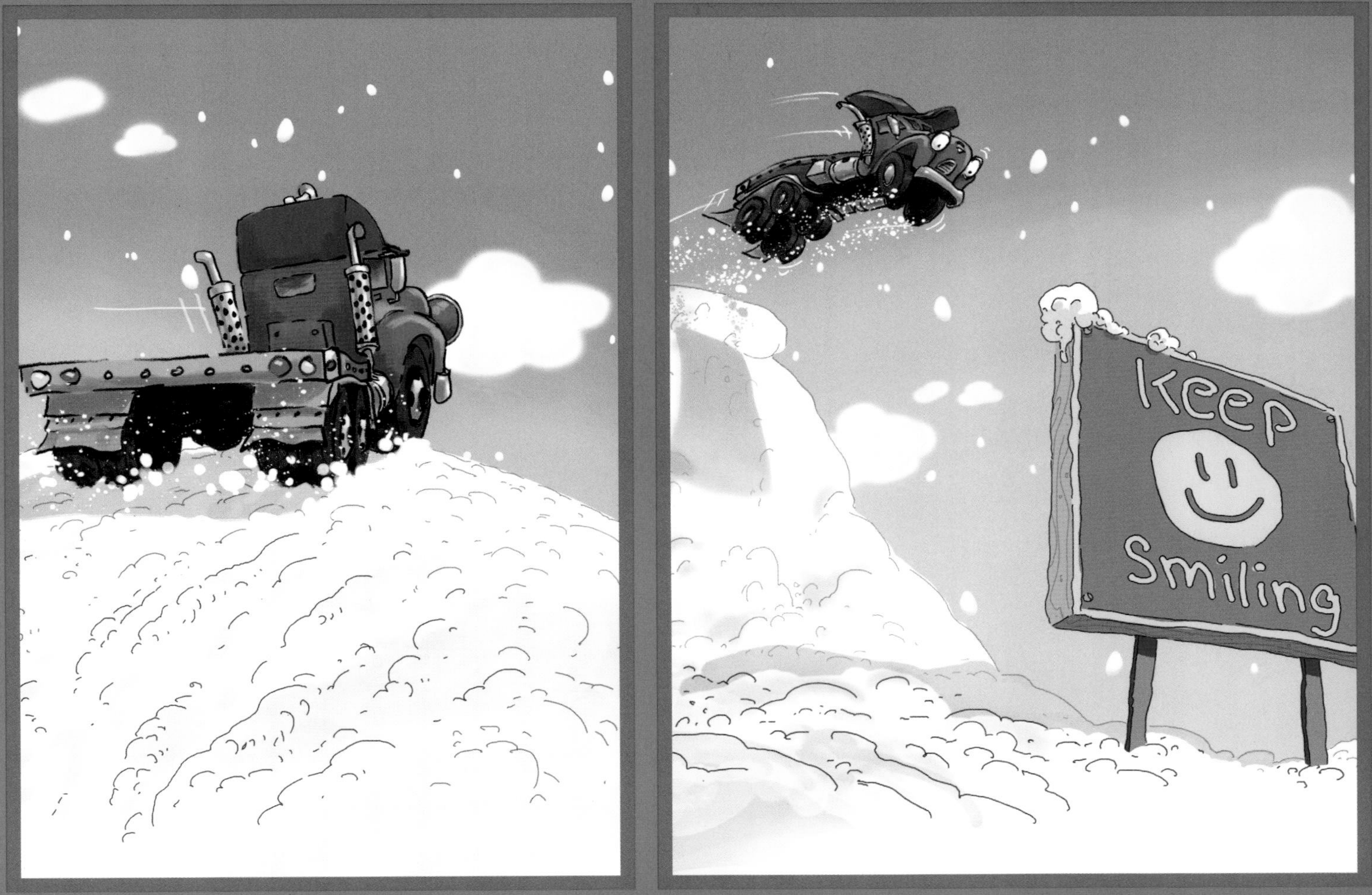
Keep
Smiling

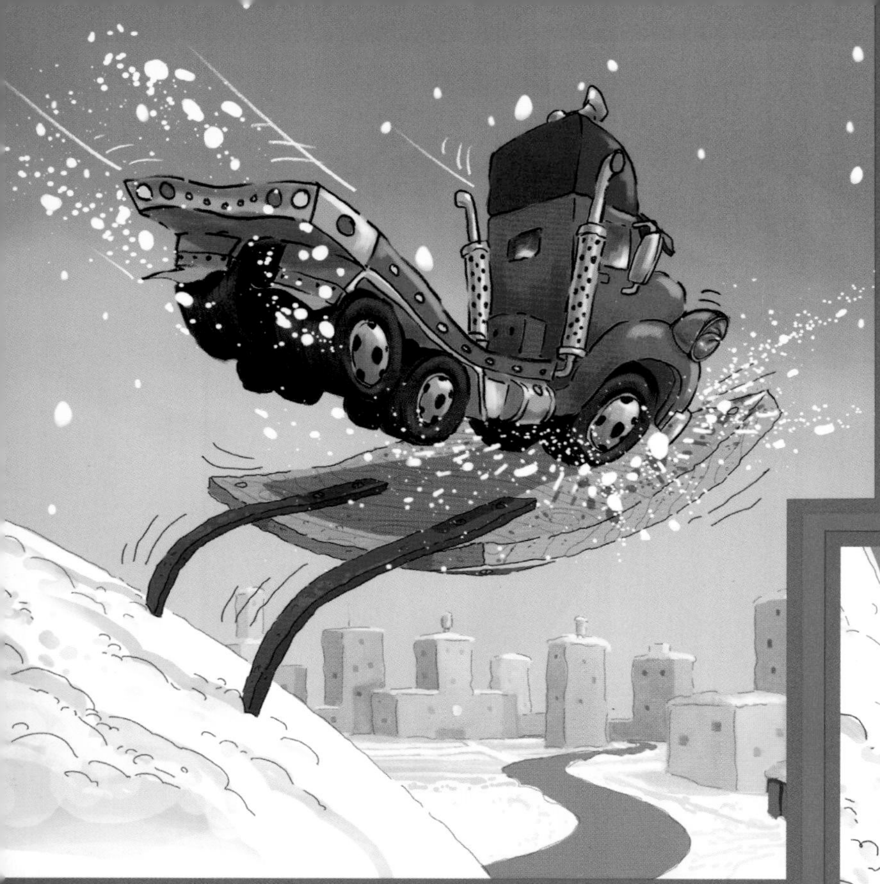

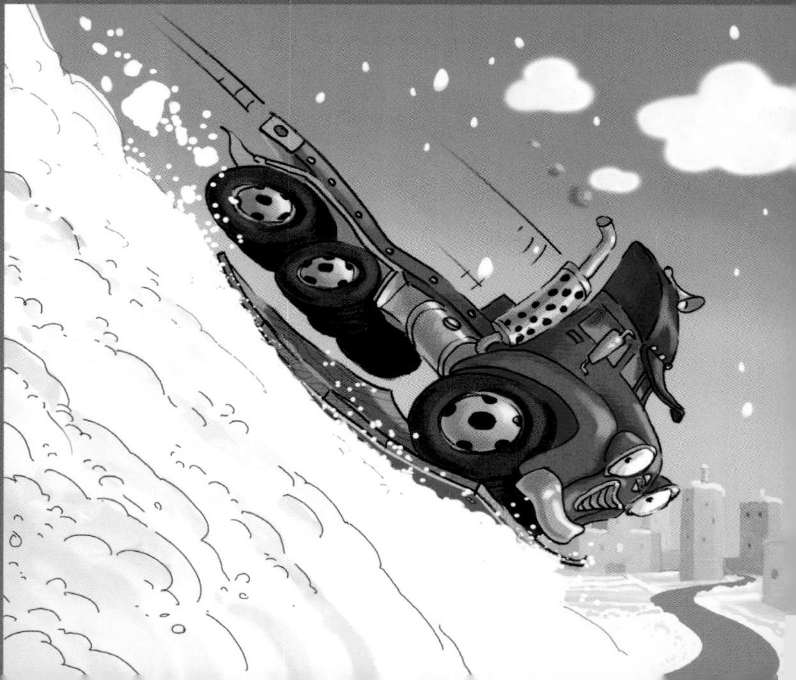

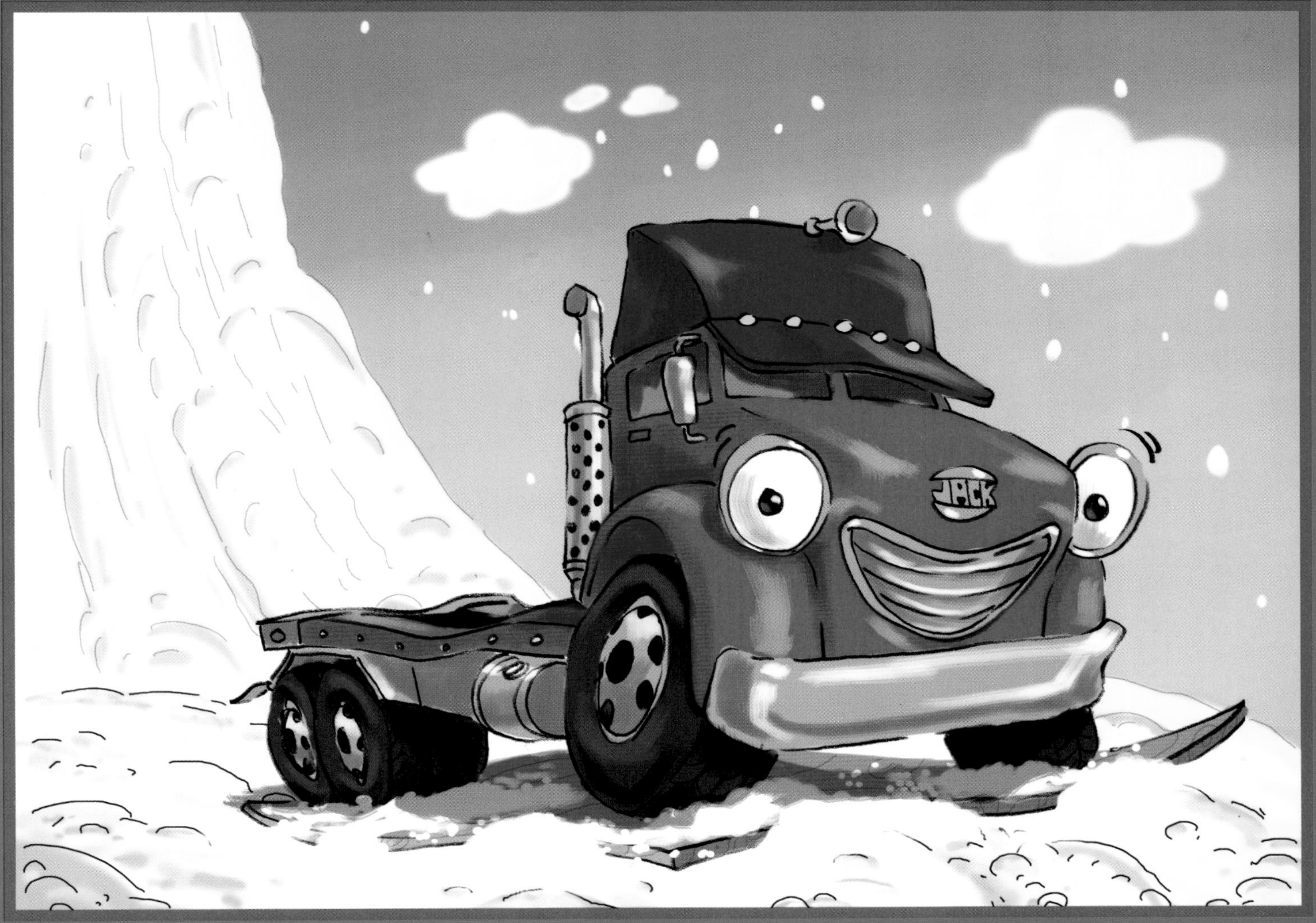
JACK

Help!

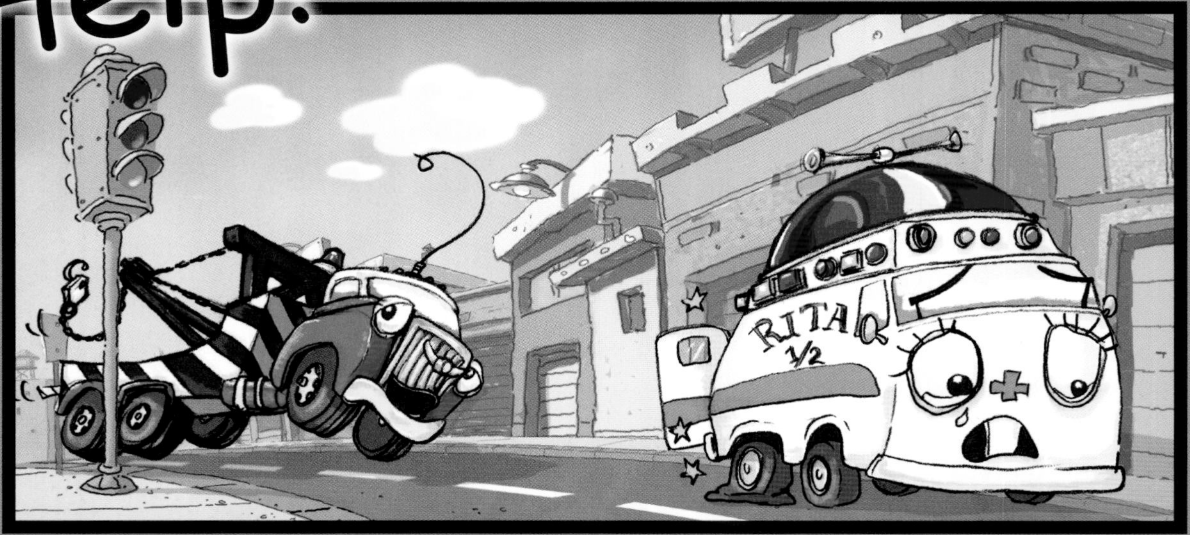

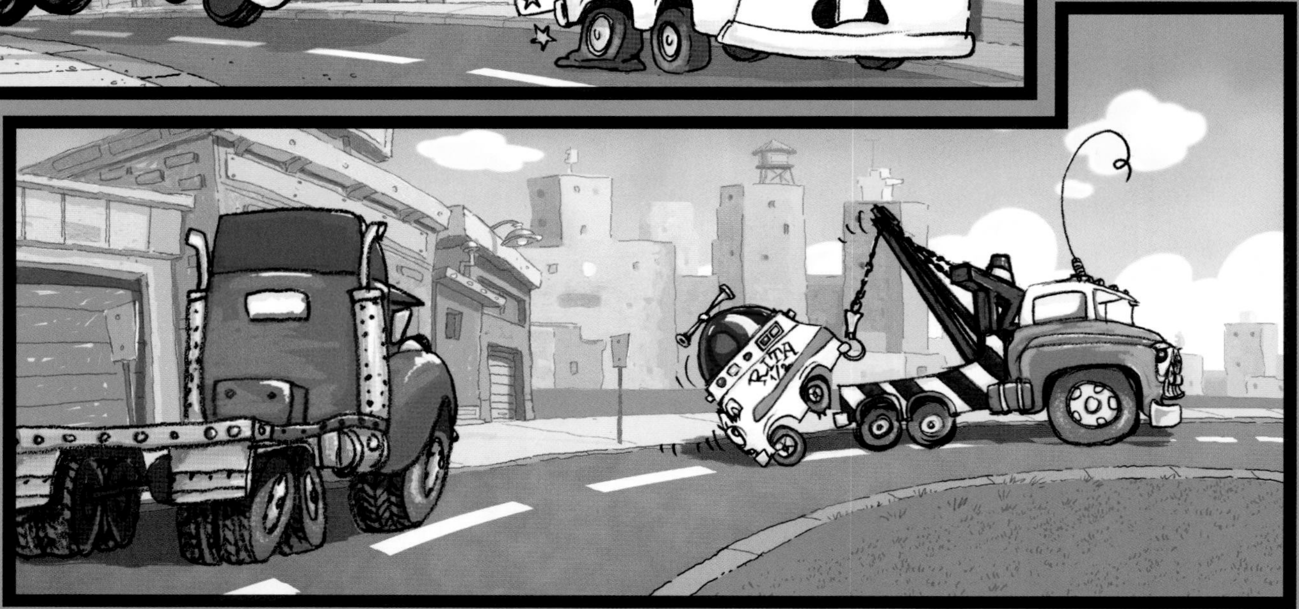

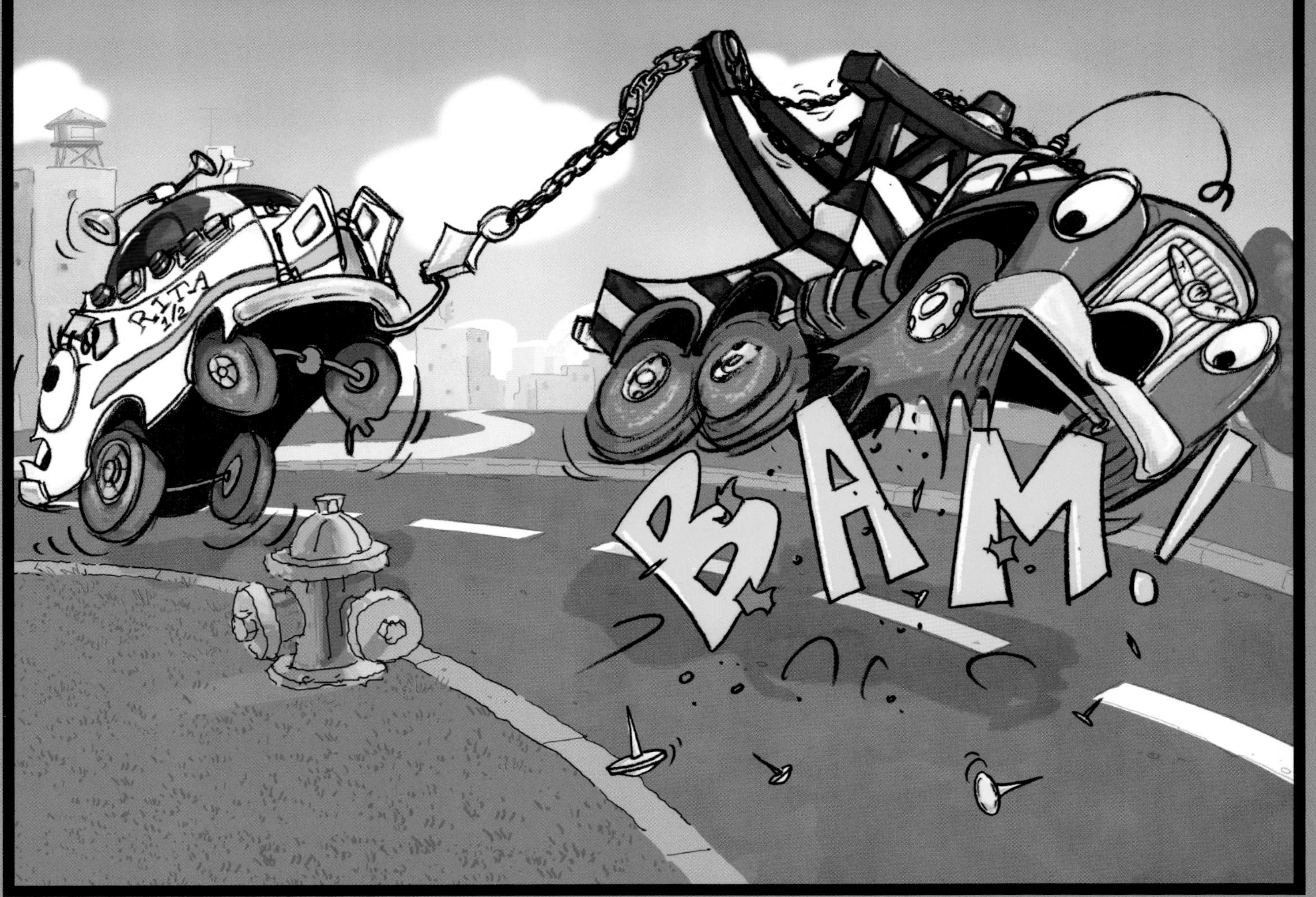
RITA 1/2
BAM!!

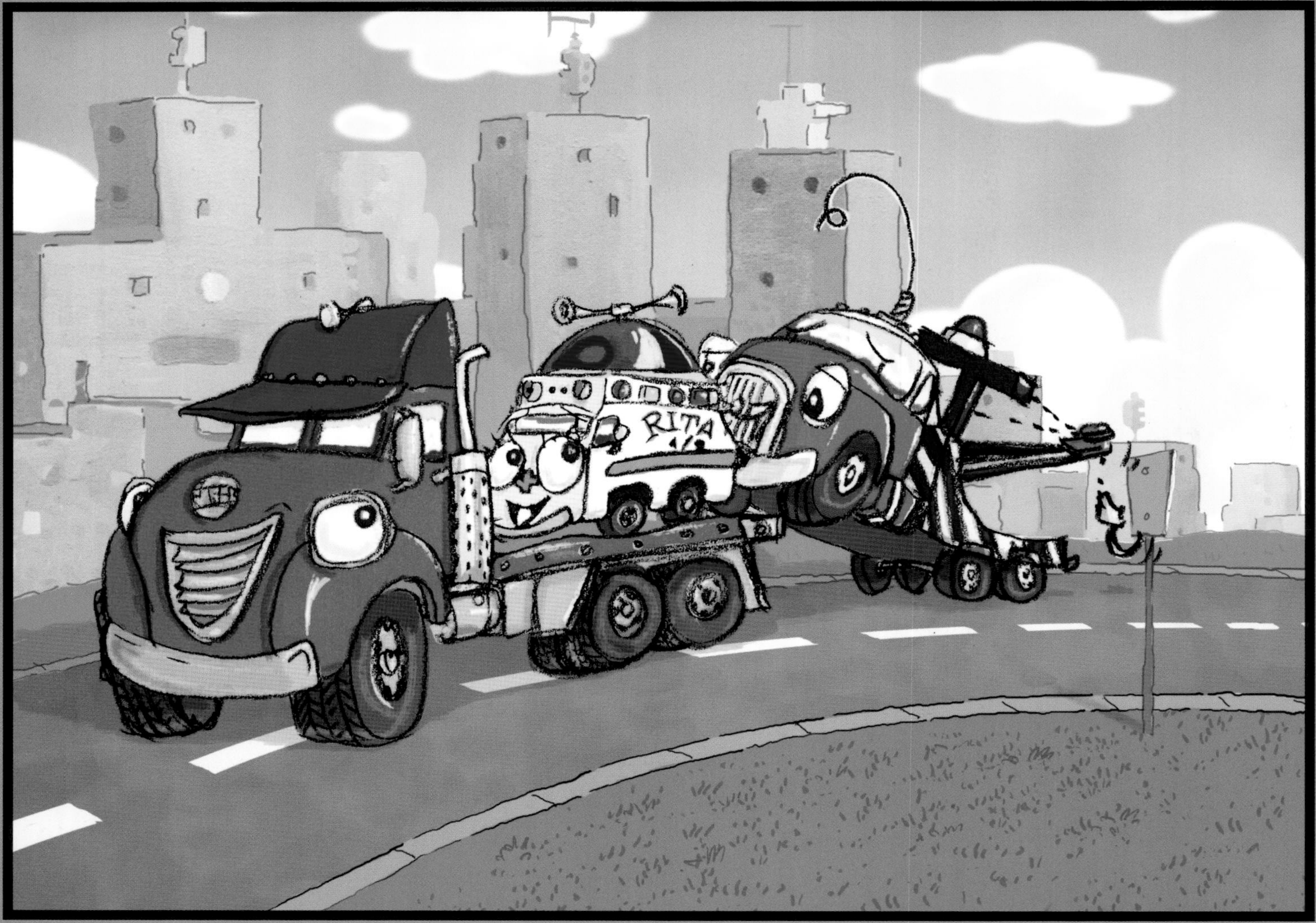
RITA